Me and My OCD

Me and My OCD

—— *My Road to Recovery* ——

Lily Françoise Millet

RESOURCE *Publications* · Eugene, Oregon

ME AND MY OCD
My Road to Recovery

Resource Publications
An Imprint of Wipf and Stock Publishers
199 W. 8th Ave., Suite 3
Eugene, OR 97401

www.wipfandstock.com

PAPERBACK ISBN: 979-8-3852-0287-4
HARDCOVER ISBN: 979-8-3852-0288-1
EBOOK ISBN: 979-8-3852-0289-8

VERSION NUMBER 12/18/23

Dedication

THIS BOOK IS DEDICATED to Sinéad O'Connor, who was like a little sister or a younger version of myself. We were conflicted about the same things—the Irish Republican Army, the hierarchy of the Church. Like me, she didn't always know what she was doing. But—she was brave, she was beautiful, and she was broken. She used her angelic voice to evoke pride in the word *Mandinka*, to condemn a *Famine* that wasn't a famine, and to presage Black Lives Matter with *Black Boys on Mopeds*. She died at age 56 on July 26, 2023. I wish you had persevered, little sister, but a part of you is still within me. If you or someone you know is considering suicide, please call the national suicide hotline at 988. I really do care about you. *We are survivors.*

Contents

Teenhood and Adulthood

Dear Paul

Dear Paul, Again

Recovery

Abbreviations

ADHD	Attention-Deficit/Hyperactivity Disorder
AIDS	Acquired Immune Deficiency Syndrome
ANTIFA	anti-fascist
CNN	Cable News Network.
COVID-19	Coronavirus Disease 2019
DACA	Deferred Action on Childhood Arrivals
ESPN	Entertainment and Sports Programming Network
ICE	Immigration and Customs Enforcement
LGBTQ	lesbian, gay, bisexual, transgender, and queer (or questioning).
MSNBC	Microsoft National Broadcasting Company
NATO	North Atlantic Treaty Organization
OCD	Obsessive Compulsive Disorder
TPS	Temporary Protected Status
USA or US	United States of America
UN	United Nations

Preface

THIS BOOK WAS PAINFUL for me to write because it brought back memories and forced me to admit embarrassing parts of my life. Yet it some ways it helped me. It was somewhat like writing in a journal. It helps record and clarify things. If you or a loved one suffers from OCD, there is help. Please contact International OCD Foundation at http://www/iocdfoundation.org. If you or a loved one is contemplating suicide, please contact the suicide hotline at 988. I hope this book is useful to the lay public, to those who suffer or have loved ones who suffer with OCD, for those who practice psychiatry and therapy, and for those who teach psychiatry or abnormal psychology and their students. If you suffer from OCD, I hope this book can also give you some comfort, some hope, and a means to recovery. I care about you.

Acknowledgements

THANK YOU TO THE kind, wise, and empathetic priest who helped me get through all this. You know who you are. I am eternally grateful.

Introduction

THE BOOK BEGINS WITH my childhood and college years; then returns back to my childhood, teen hood, and adulthood. Then, in the form of a letter to the man I married in college, I return to my childhood, the onset of my OCD and my family environment, my college and graduate school days, and our lives together after graduate school. The book ends with my recovery and my thoughts about recovery for those who bear the debilitating hopelessness and helplessness of OCD. There is truly hope!

She

Chapter 1. **She**

SHE WAS A LONELY child.

It was better that way.

Then people didn't know how stupid she was . . .

Or how much she hated herself . . .

It's not that she really *was* stupid. In fact, she was smart. But *she* didn't have a word for what she was, so she chose "stupid." She did things no one else did. She had thoughts no one else had. And she hurt in ways no one else did.

She had two friends, but she never told them about herself. She didn't tell them why she was there sometimes, and sometimes she wasn't.

She had one sister. They were close. She loved her more than anyone else. She told her very little.

At night, she cried. She cried herself to sleep. No one knew she was crying. No one even knew she was sad.

College

Chapter 2. **Leaving Home**

THERE WAS SOMETHING ABOUT leaving home for college that was a good thing. There was a sense of freedom. I was never *really* free, but this was different. It *felt* a little better. I did some things. Some normal things.

No one knew me here—no one knew what I was or what I had done. I could be whoever I wanted to be. No one knew I was making it up as I went along.

I decided to have fun. I had a friend. We were close, even though I told her very little. And I went out with boys, lots of boys. These relationships were all short-lived because I wouldn't "put out," to use the jargon of the day. That was okay, though, because like I said, I was having fun. We went out to the bars, danced to Smokey Robinson, hitchhiked home, and that was that. When one boy dumped me, I moved onto the next. It didn't really matter and I didn't really care.

The other women in the dorm were dumbfounded when they learned about my straight-A grades. I guess no one expected this from the party girl. I worked hard though. I worked all day, then went to the bars at night. I got my A's.

Chapter 3. **Vietnam**

Give peace a chance. (Title by John Lennon)[1]

I DID A LOT more than get straight A's. It is strange for me to realize that despite everything going on in my head, I was able to make some kind of a life for myself. Even before I left home for college, I was politically active. My sister reminded me that I told the customers at the supermarket where I worked that they shouldn't buy grapes during Caesar Chavez's boycott in support of migrant workers. And I hated the war in Vietnam. I read the newspaper every morning to see which side was winning. Whichever side had a higher kill count was defined as the winner that day. It went back and forth, back and forth. But everyone was suffering so much, one day more on one side, the next day more on the other.

I studied the war and the country—the history, the background, and the people. I joined an anti-war action committee and read books about Vietnam while still in high school. I read many more over the years. When I arrived in college, I majored in political science with an emphasis on Southeast Asia. If I was going to oppose a war, I was going to know as much about it as I could. I didn't know it then, but within several months my roommate would be from Vietnam. Nor did I realize that one day I would travel to Vietnam and learn even more about this

---

1. Music titles, lyrics, and musicians are cited at the end of the book in Chapter 67.

beautiful but devastated country. Nor did I know the full Pentagon Papers would eventually reveal the truths about the war that were hidden by our government.[2]

I threw myself into politics. I marched and rallied when Nixon bombed Cambodia. I was the campus coordinator for the George McGovern campaign—McGovern, the peace candidate, who lost in part to Nixon's dirty tricks. The war ended in 1975, but by then there were other global problems that had already taken my mind off the war.

2. Sheehan, *The Pentagon Papers.*

Chapter 4. **The World Food Crisis**

BY 1973, A "WORLD food crisis" caused in small part by bad weather and in large part by bad politics was in full swing. For the first time ever, we saw on television the starving children with their protruding stomachs. We saw the skeletal men who looked fifty years older than they actually were. We saw the sad, sad mothers as they watched their babies die.

I sold all my books and gathered up all the silver dollars my great uncle had given me over the years. This was all I owned in this world, and I sent it to charities for the world's poor. Believe it or not, I began to communicate with Sister (later Mother, now Saint) Theresa. I joined a national citizens' lobby that sought legislative approval for policies that would help the poor,[1] and I started a chapter of this organization at my college. Our group was active and I was busy. I was greeted by famed anthropologist Margaret Mead for my work. I made new friends—good friends—but I didn't tell them about myself. I was involved and occupied and in a sense, I was thriving. I wasn't okay, but it seemed like I was.

1. The organization, Bread for the World (www.bread.org) continues to do its excellent work today.

Chapter 5. **An Escape**

I REALIZE NOW THAT leaving home was a monumental escape. I never went back. Really—no weekend visits home even though I was only seventy miles away. No trips except for Christmas, once for a wedding reception . . . and well, there was just that one other time.

As I contemplated the problem of world hunger, I eventually concluded that economics was at its heart. I had never taken an economics course, but I decided I would earn an economics Ph.D. I applied to excellent programs at outstanding graduate schools around the country. Despite not having an economics major and having only a minor by that time, I still received offers covering full tuition and living expenses at multiple schools with exceptional programs. I chose the best one.

But that happened years later. I was still just a first-year college student. And this business about thriving . . . it came to an end when I met Paul. Paul, with whom I fell in love. Paul, with whom I couldn't get along. Paul—I couldn't be with him, and I couldn't be without him.

Chapter 6. **Paul**

THERE WAS A PARTY going on in the college recreational building and I decided to walk over. I had broken up with my current boyfriend just a few hours earlier. I had liked him but had no strong feelings about the breakup. I wondered who I would go out with next.

As I arrived at the building, Perry told me Paul was looking for me. I guess the word of my break-up had gotten around. Perry was an ex-con—tough-talking and tough-looking, my source for weed, my sort-of friend.

Paul was looking for me! Of all the boys on this side of campus, Paul was the one I had never gone out with, had never even talked to. He was different from the others, and so cool. He never went out to the bars. He had wire-rimmed glasses and long hair. He dressed in jeans and a flannel shirt and was a bit of a loner. He stood out. He was a prodigy of sorts . . . not just smart, but an amazing pianist, brilliant. He had come to college from the conservatory. And now Paul was looking for me . . .

Chapter 7. **That First Night**

WE CONNECTED. WE TALKED all night. I never knew that talking with someone could be such a thrill. Getting to know that person even though I thought I knew so many people before! I even told him some things about myself. Carefully, cautiously . . . safe things. We liked the same books—the "cool" authors of the era: Herman Hesse, Alan Watts, and Kurt Vonnegut. We both played piano and loved Mozart and Bach. We liked the same popular music. Cat Stevens (Yusuf)—*It's a Wild World*. Led Zeppelin—*Stairway to Heaven*. Neil Young—*Don't Let it Bring you Down*. The Beatles—*Let it Be*. Then there was Laura Nyro: "Gonna kill . . . my Lover-Man." I loved her album, with her beautiful voice constantly on the verge of a scream.

And, of course, there was Bread. Paul sang *If* to me—with his classical guitar. *If* became *our* song. Our first night together, alone in his dorm room, him sneaking me into the bathroom, me meeting old boyfriends along the way. Our first night was innocent. And it was full of wonder!

We walked together in the woods the next day. Again, we talked. By then, we knew we were soulmates, destined to be together.

I would never be lonely again.

Chapter 8. **Happiness Ended**

AND THAT'S WHEN MY bit of happiness ended. It happened slowly. Petty arguments. Small criticisms. Then bigger disagreements. Tears. Loud words. Shouting. People watching. People always watching. People watching when we ate together, when we studied together, the time I slapped his face without even realizing it . . . They were always watching.

Everyone knew, and they must have been talking. *What is wrong with them*, they must have asked.

I isolated myself from everyone else. I was never that social anyway, except for the superficial times with the boys. I worried. I cried. I waited for his phone call. And then, the call, the voice I loved, the voice I craved, both of us making up, and the overwhelming relief of reconciliation. The daily reunion after the daily fight. I thought that I loved him. I *did* love him, and he *did* love me, but it was never a healthy love. We were bound together by something real, but also something sick—a kind of mutual dependency.

I was unwell. The dependency was just an added layer, since the old days had never really left me. I was wearing camouflage. I hid my real self very well—even from myself.

Chapter 9. **The Counsellors**

I WAS LOSING THE bearings I had gained in a new place with new people and experiences. Campus counsellors took note. They said they would help me, but only if I agreed to end my relationship with Paul. They shouldn't have forced me to choose. I needed their help. They refused to help me and I refused them. They were wrong and I was wrong. I chose the relationship.

I continued my deep distraught each time we "broke up" and my utter relief each time we made up again. It happened over and over. I tried to hide it—the sadness and the tears, but everyone knew.

I coped poorly. I began drinking when I felt hopeless. I *always* felt hopeless. I drank when I felt desperate. I *always* felt desperate. Hopeless and desperate. Hopeless and helpless. I bashed my fist through glass windows. I rode my bike through traffic in the dark while blinded by my tears. I climbed to high places and then I jumped down. I fantasized about running into traffic. I put away knives because they were too tempting. I locked the car door so I couldn't jump out.

I found myself lying in the rain on the campus grounds one night. I was crying and screaming. I didn't even realize how wretched I was and how awful it looked. A boy came by and asked if I was okay. I was embarrassed. I got up, I said *yes*, but meant *no.* Then I walked home.

Chapter 10. **The Homecoming**

As I SAID, ASIDE from Christmas and the wedding reception, there was just one time I went back to my parents' house during college. Paul and I had fought. Loud and angry and tears and screaming . . . I called my dad and asked him to pick me up and bring me home, and he did—no questions asked. We never spoke of it while we drove in the car. And when we got home, we all sat in the back yard—my mom and dad, my sister Jodie and her boyfriend—and I told them I needed to be hospitalized. I was ill and I couldn't go on. The response? No one responded. No one answered. No one talked about it. No one said a word. I went back to college the next day. It was all as if nothing had happened, as if nothing had been said. But it was real . . .

My Childhood

Chapter 11. **The Family We Lived With**

WE DIDN'T HAVE MUCH family in the United States since we were from Canada. But our family was close to another family that welcomed us into their home when we arrived in America. They and my parents remained close all their lives, like an extended dysfunctional family. I later came to believe that the mom, Evelyn, was a sociopath, and I know she mistreated her children. Her mother, Zelda, was the shrill ugly witch her name resembled. The dad, Thomas, was a drunk. The kids were damaged beyond repair. Like me.

Jodie and I played "war" with the boy our age. His name was Sam. In case you don't know, war is a card game. It requires absolutely no thought and can take hours or even days to play. Over the years, my sister and I have run into Sam a few times. He is a bit off, just as he has always been. I suspect his mom damaged him deeply.

The oldest boy, Jamie, end up divorced after abusing his wife. The oldest girl, Sheila, ended up marrying a man who refused to let her visit her family. She could only work in her home beauty-shop and she was lucky he let her do that.

I mention all this about Evelyn and Thomas and their family because after we moved out of their home, we still lived only fifteen miles away. We visited them often, especially every Christmas. My dad and Thomas would drink, a lot—rum and cokes. My sister and I huddled together behind a couch and we played with our many gifts from Evelyn, especially our dolls. On the ride home, we sat in the back seat of the car in the dark, terrified we would fly off one of the curves on the highway and tumble down to our deaths. We didn't have seat belts in those days, and our parents always smoked in the car. And, of course, they were drunk. I guess we never told our parents how frightened we were. Our mother was surprised to hear us tell her the story when we were adults.

Chapter 12. **The Family We Were Related To**

OUR ONLY REAL RELATIVES in America were my mother's Uncle Jed and his wife, Aunt Amy. Jodie and I hated our visits to their home, which was required of us regularly. They had a frightful German shepherd that even my mom was afraid of. My dad and Uncle Jed would split a big bottle of whiskey and quickly become very drunk. They thought it was funny when they bought each other identical bottles of Canadian whisky for Christmas—well, Uncle Jed thought it was funny and my dad just pretended. Uncle Jed was loud and stupid and racist, though Aunt Amy was nice to Jodie and me. Poor Aunt Amy, married to that obnoxious man. She was constantly asking him not to be so loud. When he laughed, he hollered "hee, hee, hee" in a high-pitched garish voice. Whenever he phoned my mother, his voice boomed across the house. My mother would hold the phone far from her ear to temper the volume. Jodie and I didn't like him, but Aunt Amy was okay. Aunt Amy eventually became senile and lived in a nursing home near Jodie's house. She became even sweeter as she aged, and we liked her more and more.

Aunt Amy's elderly mother lived with Aunt Amy and Uncle Jed when Jodie and I were little. Poor woman—I don't even know her name. I think we called her Grandma Moss. Uncle Jed always hollered *Gertie* at her, but I know that wasn't her real name. This great, great aunt had dementia. Her senility frightened Jodie, and it made me uncomfortable. Regardless, Jodie and I were required to sit with her and keep her company whenever we visited. She always told us the same old story, about the dog that followed her to school and waited for her there until school was done. She *loved* to tell us that story, over and over.

Grandma Moss once stayed with us in our home so Uncle Jed and Aunt Amy could take a holiday. She wanted to wash dishes, but my mother wouldn't let her. One day we found her washing the dishes in the toilet.

The only saving grace about our visits to Uncle Jed was the ice-cold soda pop he kept for us in the basement and the silver dollars he gave us. The basement had a musty odor that I can almost smell as I write this. As always, we had the terrifying ride home, Jodie and I frightened in the back seat as our drunken dad drove us home.

Chapter 13. **Waiting for my Mother**

I DON'T REMEMBER MY symptoms setting in until I was around seven years old, and they started out mild. My earlier memories were the embarrassing but normal things of very young childhood, like when Sheila took a bunch of us little kids for a walk and I wet my pants. Or, when I wore my pajama bottoms under my skirt to kindergarten by mistake, and my mom's friend laughed at me when she noticed. I remember getting sick to my stomach on a swing, and for some reason, I recall the time I picked up what I thought was a belt that turned out to be a dead snake. I thought the girl in the park was the daughter of a king because her last name was King. Susan King. Aside from these, I remember little else except the time I spent alone.

My mummy worked night shifts at the hospital as a nurse. We called her mummy then, because we hadn't yet learned that American school kids said "mommy" or "mom." When I say, "we," I am always referring to my sister, Jodie. We were almost always together.

Still, I was so lonely when my mummy slept during the day. I would sit outside her closed bedroom door for hours. I often sat on a rug with a pile of her jewelry, and I pretended I was on a magic carpet. I don't remember where Jodie was or what she was doing. Maybe she was napping. But I do remember my mummy being soft and warm and pretty when she tucked us into bed at night.

Chapter 14. **Waiting for my Father**

A FEW YEARS LATER, I would sit by the front window, waiting for my dad to come home from work. Straight down the block was a bar, and I could see his large work van whenever he stopped there. Each day I hoped and prayed that he wouldn't stop, but he always did. Then I would pray that he wouldn't stay long, maybe just for one drink. But he stayed, and stayed, and was drunk by the time he got home. I stayed away from him then.

There was one time as a child that I asked him not to drink anymore. I don't remember actually doing that, but I remember Sam's older brother, Jamie, telling my sister and me how lucky we were because our dad would do anything for us. I knew that wasn't true because I somehow knew I had asked him. I never brought it up again until I was a grown woman, pregnant with my second child and at risk for miscarriage. I was visiting my parents and my dad was grilling meat outside. A visit meant a party, and a party meant getting drunk. In his slobbery tone, he asked me to get him another drink. I said I wasn't comfortable being with him when he was drinking. I don't know where I got the courage to broach the "forbidden" topic. Or maybe it was simple longing. He looked at me and said, *I guess you'll have to be uncomfortable then.* I left and took a long, frenzied walk—crying and worrying that I was endangering my unborn child. My dad would never have been so unkind if he hadn't been drunk. My sober dad wasn't like that. I worried until the day he died that he would cause a drunk driving accident, killing everyone involved. It would be all my fault because I was never able to stop him from drinking.

Chapter 15. **Good Times with My Dad**

I've HEARD THAT WATCHING television with your child is not an effective bonding strategy.

Nevertheless, it worked for me and my dad. We *did* have our good times. We had our favorite TV shows and we faithfully watched them together, especially *Bonanza, Gunsmoke,* and *Mission Impossible.* We had our own code words, and we would often speak in the manner of the characters in the shows. (Remember Festus? He was our favorite.)

My mom didn't watch TV. She just liked the noise.

Sometimes my dad and I did jigsaw puzzles. Other times, he would slice and peel apples or crack open hickory nuts for me. Occasionally, we got up early and went to gather hickory nuts in the ditches along the country roads. Just me and my dad. I liked those times with him. These are good memories. He was never drunk at those times. This is the dad I remember when I comfort myself by wearing his old flannel pajamas.

I knew my dad had repeatedly run away from home as a child, and while still underage, he kept trying to join the Canadian navy. Finally, they let him join, even though he was only seventeen. I imagine they just gave in.

My Dad was at Normandy and was so very young. He was stationed on a minesweeper, designed to sweep away or detonate explosive mines so they wouldn't endanger allied troops and their warships. I'm sure he was terrified. I suspect the older Navy men were a wild bunch. They told my dad he could cure his vomiting by eating chocolate bars and drinking Coca Cola. Of course, this made it worse. My dad had a huge scar down along his left side. He always told us a cannibal bit him. I suspected something far more realistic but perhaps more sinister.

Still, those tough navy men played solitaire in their free time, and they made paper boats and airplanes that would someday delight their children. My Dad taught me to play solitaire and how to make the paper toys. Nowadays, I sleep with my computer. When I can't sleep, I play online solitaire. It makes me feel close to my Dad. Just like when I wear his flannel pajamas.

Chapter 16. **Good Times with My Mom**

As I said, my mom was soft and warm when she tucked us into bed at night. I remember one night when she moved one of our toys in a silly way and we all laughed and giggled. And I remember the pretty dresses she wore to her parties. She also took good care of us—fed us, bought us clothing, put us to bed.

One time she told us about her childhood. She grew up in a farmhouse with six other children. Her parents worked hard, as did the kids. They lived on a farm on a prairie in the midst of the great depression. The never-ending dust storms kept everything dirty. She told us a little about their poverty: their ketchup sandwiches and homemade clothes. How her mother eventually had to take in boarders.

My mom's skin was dark, like the local Indigenous (First Nation) people. Her older brothers laughed at her and called her "injun." They told her that her tongue was too big. She always believed she was ugly.

My mom's father died when she was just in her teens. She never told us much about him, except that he was quiet and kind, very much unlike his brother, Uncle Jed. When her mother began to take in boarders, there entered my dad.

My dad had left home and boarded with my mother's family. He and my mother's mom got along well. She always said he was her favorite. But my dad and my mom's older brothers were wild, running around and drinking. Still, my dad was so damn cute, and all my mom's sisters were hoping he'd like them the best. He chose my mom. I think for the first time in her life, my mother realized how pretty she was.

I guess that's about it. I know she tried to be a good mom.

Chapter 17. **The Parties**

MY MOM LOVED HER parties! She loved to socialize. She loved to dance. And she loved to drink. She and my dad went out several evenings every week. I forgot about this until recently, when I found an old diary in which I had written down what happened day to day. One day they went to a party. The next day they went out to play cards. The next day they went out to dinner. Then they maybe skipped a day, and then there would be another party. The photos taken at parties always showed my mom sitting on somebody's lap, someone who wasn't my dad. But now, as I look through those old photos again, I see that *all* the women were sitting on somebody's lap, someone who wasn't their husband, including the women sitting on the lap of my dad.

I didn't understand why my mom kept going to parties with my dad, because he always got drunk. I hated his drinking. I thought of him as two different people—one was my nice, quiet, usually gentle dad and the other was the drunk. When he was the drunk, he wasn't my dad. I could be as rude and mean to him as I wanted. I didn't like him and I didn't like being around him.

He wasn't a violent drunk, but a slobbery one. I could see it coming as his face went slack and his eyes got watery. He became all huggy and kissy. When we went out for dinner, he called the waitress "little honey," as if he thought he was cool. When I was a bit older, I noticed how he and the neighborhood drunks shared google eye looks when they saw a pretty daughter of one of the drunks, girls that were my own age. I found it all disgusting.

My mom enabled my father's drinking, just like she enabled the smoking that eventually killed him. She believed him when he said he had quit smoking, even though *everyone* know he smoked like a fiend. She also denied his alcoholism. I understand now why she went out with him, knowing he would became so drunk—her social life was just so important to her. And, of course, she too liked to drink.

Chapter 18. **Laughing at Me**

MY SISTER AND I were very little at that early time, and we often didn't have a babysitter. I lay awake terrified every night when my parents were gone, in contrast to Jodie who immediately fell asleep. But I heard all the little outside noises, plus the louder noise made by teenagers walking past our bedroom window on their way to some fun. I was so afraid they would get us before our parents came home.

Every night when my parents returned, they were fighting. Not physically—but verbally. My dad especially got loud and angry because, of course, he was drunk. Jodie slept right through it, but my parents fought until my dad stormed down to the basement, probably for a night cap (he had a bar downstairs), and then I could hear him snoring loudly as he fell asleep on the basement sofa.

I remember worrying that my mom must be sad about all this, and though I was little, I would get up to see if she were okay. There she would be, reading the newspaper at the kitchen table. She mostly read the obituaries. She would laugh at me when I asked if she was sad. It felt to me like a huge intense event had occurred, with my dad yelling and all. It seemed it would create strong sad feelings, but my mom denied them. This was confusing for me. But then, in our house, we didn't admit to unhappy things, or "maudlin things" as my mom would say. I would hug my mom "good night," and she said, "you already hugged me."

My sister didn't mind my dad's drinking. She slept easily, instantly, as soon as our parents left to go out. She slept through their homecomings when they were fighting. I, on the other hand, lay awake the entire time, waiting for them to come home and listening to them once they arrived. So, Jodie never heard the fights—she never worried that our mother might be sad. She was never confused when our mother laughed and said *of course she wasn't sad!*

Jodie and I have different memories. We were close in age and together all the time, but we remember things so differently. I think this is mostly because she slept while I lay awake.

Chapter 19. **Jodie**

OUR PARENTS NEVER PAID much attention to us, which meant Jodie and I could do whatever we wanted. When we were little, we loved to play with our dolls—Barbie dolls, baby dolls, paper dolls, big dolls, little dolls—we played with them all for days at a time. And we played unending games of monopoly and mindless games of war.

When we weren't at home, we went to the park and played on the swings. Our favorite game was "crash derby." This is where we would swing like crazy and try to ram each other off the swing. That never happened. We never got hurt and never had bad feelings. We played a similar game when we went swimming. We took turns riding on one another's back, and without using our hands, we each hung on for dear life while the other one tried to knock us off.

Jodie and I were also TV fans and watched the same movies every year: *The Bird Man of Alcatraz; The Good, the Bad, and the Ugly; The Bad Seed; The Birds;* and of course, *The Wizard of Oz.* (I swear we can recite all the lines of the *Wizard of Oz.*) We had different tastes in TV shows, so we took turns—Jodie's game shows and my, well, sort of nerdy shows: *The Waltons, Leave it to Beaver,* and even *Father Knows Best.* Jodie's favorite show was the *Newly Wed Game* with host Bob Eubanks (I think she had a little crush on him). And now, I just remembered another show: *Queen for a Day.* What a sick and sad show—women competing with their melancholy stories for a prize that went to the one with the most wretched life. I can't imagine people watching a comparable show with men as the contestants!

Then the Beatles arrived and we watched them on the *Ed Sullivan Show*. We thought they had to be wearing wigs, as we had never seen men with hair that long! But we were mesmerized, as was everyone else. The girls in the audience screamed and cried and fainted and I'd never before seen such a sensation.

Jodie and I knew *all* the lyrics to *all* the songs and not just those of the Beatles. So along with *All My Loving* and *She Loves You*, we sang *California Dreaming, Downtown, I've Got You Babe, Mrs. Brown You've Got a Lovely Daughter, I'm Henry the Eighth I Am*, and everything else that was popular at the time. We sang while we did the dishes. I couldn't wash, so Jodie washed and I dried. She was good like that. I couldn't vacuum, so she vacuumed and I dusted.

Jodie knew about my mental anguish, and I would often ask for her reassurance. She gave it unquestionably, and she never yelled or made me feel stupid.

Chapter 20. **Our Mom's Denial**

MY MOM REFUSED TO believe I had a mental illness. She refused to believe my dad was an alcoholic or a smoker. She denied that she was ever sad. Jodie and I were not allowed to be sad or talk about unhappy matters. If we were overheard talking quietly together, my mom would say, "You're not being maudlin, are you?" That was her word, *maudlin*. My mom's mixed signals about what we should feel were confusing for me as a child.

Jodie recently reminded me that not only were we not allowed to *be* sad, but our mom regularly told us we were *not* sad, even when we knew we were. *She literally told us our feelings were incorrect!*

And my mom didn't like anyone who was different—it didn't matter how or why. Handicapped. Gay. Slow. Unhappy. Yes, unhappy! Remember, we were not supposed to be *maudlin*. We were supposed to be happy and well-adjusted and sociable and definitely and entirely without any mental illness. I don't think she ever watched it, but she wouldn't have liked the women on *Queen for a Day!* She would have told them they weren't really sad and they should just get on with their lives!

Teenhood and Adulthood
Chapter 21. **Politics and Noise**

THERE WAS A TIME when my dad worked briefly for Dow Chemical Company. Maybe we needed some extra money. We never talked of politics in our house. There were *lots* of things we didn't talk about, but still I knew my dad was more liberal than my mom. He was a tradesman—a journeyman plumber—and hence a union supporter. Dow Chemical would turn out to be a bit controversial.

My mom had no concept of political ideology. She would ask me the difference between conservative and liberal, and I would explain in terms of less vs. more government. She never remembered and would ask me again and again. I would write it down for her, but that didn't help. Instinctively, though, she was a full-blown conservative. She loved conservative talk show radio. She would later love Ronald Reagan, partly because he kindly called his wife "Mommie." I unkindly called him "Ronnie" because he slashed our nation's poverty programs and referred to Black women as welfare queens.

My mom was truly enamored with those conservative talk shows. We could never speak or make any noise while they were turned on. It was as if she couldn't cope if she missed a single word. The radio was on everywhere in the house, and it was loud. In the car, the noise was unbearable.

It wasn't just talk radio, but all the other noise. There was a radio or television turned on in every room in the house, no matter the time of day or the program. The noise was blaring and disjointed. I suspect that all this noise somehow calmed my mom. Maybe it helped her sort out things in her head. For the rest of us, it was a horrible nerve-wracking noisy abomination.

After I left home, I would sometimes forget about all the noise. I'd be jarred from what was likely self-preservation amnesia whenever I returned for a visit. Realizing what was happening, I went straight to my old room and closed the door. It was rude, but I couldn't bear the noise. My dad also hated my mom's talk shows, but he didn't tell me this until many years later.

My dad did bring up politics with me just one time, the time of Dow Chemical. He mentioned to me that I must be upset about him working there. After all, Dow was responsible for napalm, which was burning the Vietnamese people and their environment.

I don't think I answered him, and I know we didn't talk about it, but yes, I was upset.

Chapter 22. What Happened to Our Mother

SEEMINGLY OVERNIGHT, OUR WARM soft mummy turned into a hard cold bitch. I'm sorry to say this so abruptly, but it *was* abrupt and it caught us off guard. And I apologize for using a word that sounds so harsh, but it is the only word that fit her. I think part of it was menopause. She screamed when she had a hot flash. She ripped off most of her clothes and lay on the living room sofa. It lasted most of the rest of her life and my sister and I felt the brunt of it.

My mom had a schedule and a structure to housecleaning, and we had to clean the house *just right*. Every dust ball, every crumb. It freaked her out when we threw our dirty socks into the laundry inside-out, and she made us give her back our allowance whenever we did this. Fortunately, she had to do the laundry herself, because she had a convoluted system that no one else could follow. She spent more time with the laundry than anyone I've ever known. And when we finished our chores, she mostly criticized and complained. She mostly criticized me.

My mom refused to throw out food. She wouldn't let it go to waste. She used her old ingredients for baking, apparently to "mask" the bad taste of bad ingredients. She forced us to eat freezer-burned ice cream before she would buy us anymore that was fresh. I sometimes dream of the horrible taste it left in my mouth. My sister and I had the job of tasting crackers from every box to make sure they weren't stale for the guests at her parties.

Then she used the old crackers to make us an odd sort of apple pie that didn't include apples.

The cruelest way she used up old food was to place it in front of my sister when Jodie was on the telephone. Jodie had the habit of eating whatever was in front of her while she was talking with friends. And then, our mom would tell my sister she was fat. I imagine this damaged Jodie's self-esteem to the point she over-ate.

Everything I did seemed to bother my mom. Apparently I had a habit of licking my lips. I wouldn't have even known this except she constantly pointed it out. (I'm licking my lips as I write this.) And she hated my hair, always asking when I would "do something" with it. I remember visiting her as an adult, and the first thing she said was, "I see you haven't done anything with your hair yet." No wonder *I* had no self-esteem either.

It wasn't just that our mother didn't like us. She always talked about how much she liked our cousins and friends, none of whom were fat or had a mental illness. They were so cute. They set the table so nicely. They knew how to arrange the food so attractively. They dressed so beautifully. They knew how to shop. *Yikes, mom, is that what it takes for you to like us?* These superficial things?

There was something else that haunted me even more than my mom's emotionally-abusive behavior. Why didn't our dad protect us from her? Tell her to stop. Make her leave us alone. My dad was normally kind, so this has always mystified me. Maybe he was afraid of her.

Chapter 23. **The Crazy Part**

JODIE AND I HAVE the same conversation whenever we're together. It is automatic, because our lives at that point had become so very strange. Everyone in town knew our mother, and they all thought highly of her. Whenever we went anywhere with her, whether it was shopping or to church or anywhere else, we knew we would run into people she knew and they would talk and talk. Jodie and I just stood there . . . and stood there and stood there. Our mother gave no thought to our discomfort. And it was never ending. Our mom was sociable and chatty, plus she knew *just* how to solve everyone's problems. She told them in depth and without any reluctance. That made us crazy, but everyone else seemed to love it. Everyone else seemed to love *her*!

Jodie and I, on the other hand, were shy and never knew how to act or what to say. I always felt bad for my mom, that she had such dumb, stupid daughters. We just stood there, being entirely and stupidly unsociable.

Here's the really crazy part. *All* these people *always* told us how lucky we were to have our wonderful mother! Were they talking about *our* mother, the bitch?! We just looked at each other in bewilderment. As I said, we still talk about it to this day, how very strange that all was. In fact, it's the first and last thing we talk about whenever we get together.

Do you remember how I wondered why our dad didn't intervene to protect us? Jodie told me her theory about this. She believes our dad couldn't stand our mother's bitching any more than we could. So, he would try to escape, either by drinking, golfing, engaging in hobbies, or in any way he could. Jodie also believes he encouraged her drinking because she was nicer when she did.

Chapter 24. **A Memory of my Mother**

LAST NIGHT I REMEMBERED something about my mother that occurred a bit later in my life. She and my dad were living in their "Florida winter home" when Jodie and I and all our kids decided to drive there and to visit. Between the five kids, their ages must have been from around four through ten. As soon as we arrived, the kids ran to my mom's refrigerator. Kids—I thought—looking for food! But when I came closer, I saw they were all reading the expiration dates on everything in the fridge. I laugh as I remember this, because to the best of my knowledge, Jodie and I had never talked to them or around them about their grandmother's penchant for keeping old food.

Chapter 25. **My Dad**

MANY YEARS AFTER I left home, I tried an alcoholic intervention with my dad. The odds were stacked against me, since I did it all by myself. No one else, except for Paul, believed my dad was an alcoholic. I read various books on interventions, and following their directions, I wrote him a letter (since I lived too far away to talk with him in person). I told him what I didn't like about his drinking—how it affected me, how it affected my kids, and what my biggest fears were. My mom and dad took the letter badly. My mom held it against me most of my remaining life, and my dad later told me he read it, threw it away, and never thought about it again. He said that in an effort to be kind. Neither of them ever got the point.

Not long after the letter, my dad was diagnosed with cancer. I needed to apologize if I wanted to feel okay being with him throughout the dying process. I didn't tell him it was an attempted intervention. Instead, I took back everything I had said in the letter and I told him I didn't mean any of it. I told him all my happy memories of him from my childhood. We were fine together then, although granted, my intervention was a monumental failure. My mom, however, couldn't get over it. She told me repeatedly for many more years that one should always wait to cool off before sending an angry letter. *She really didn't get it.* When I finally explained it many years later, that I wasn't angry or upset when I wrote it and it was my attempt at an intervention, she appeared stunned. And oddly enough, she had nothing to say.

My dad's doctor gave him nine months to live. I was with him when we heard this. It was no surprise to me, but he was shocked. My mom must have convinced him there was nothing wrong. And, she had planned a party with friends for the time of our arrival home from the clinic. It was such an important time to talk about our feelings, such a powerful time to address our concerns. But my mom knew instinctively that she couldn't do it. Our feelings would have to wait. We had a party to go to. My dad got drunk, my mom socialized, and I just slumped away.

My mom refused to believe the diagnosis. She believed they would continue to live a long and happy life. She convinced him to agree with her. They planned on buying a new home and estate. My dad drove me there so I could see it, and as so often was the case, I was baffled but I said nothing. My mom was planning extended vacation trips for them. Our Canadian relatives were confused and sought information from me. I was forced to explain. *No, he will not live long. No, they will not be traveling. No, it will not be a long and happy life.*

Chapter 26. **A Dream**

I HAD A DREAM about my dad. I knew it was him even though he was only five years old in my dream.

I had received a call from some "authority," who told me I needed to dispatch to Canada immediately. There was a little boy halfway up the stadium bleachers and he refused to come down. They needed me to bring him down.

I went to him and I held him in my arms. We talked quietly for a very long time. We cried. And then he came down, and they made him go back home to his stepmother.

My dad was born in 1926. His family was poor and the times were hard, just like they were for my mom and her family. We couldn't learn too much from the news clipping we found, only that his mother died when my dad was a baby. This was something he never talked about, and even my mom didn't know he had had a baby brother who died along with his mother. This baby must have been close in age to our father. We don't know which baby was older, and we don't know who died first, the mother or baby. We can only imagine a great deal of sadness.

My dad's father couldn't take care of him alone. His family had been pioneers to the desolate Canadian prairie, and now he delivered coal to customers in a horse-drawn carriage from dawn to dusk. But my dad's deceased mother had sisters and these sisters adored my dad. They took him in, cared for him, and spoiled him entirely. All was good, until my dad's father remarried, and to the wicked stepmother no less. His father took him home with them, where this highly "Christian" stepmother abused him, physically and emotionally. I don't know the details, but I knew my father regularly ran away from home and was punished severely for it. Then his stepmother gave birth to another son, the perfect son in contrast with my father. Someday, the perfect son would have perfect children, also in contrast to my father. Jodie and I were not perfect children—compared to them, we felt so *stupid*. They, on the other hand, were talented, well-adjusted, and never maudlin. They were neither mentally ill nor fat. My mom adored them.

I like to think that by helping my dad in my dream, I somehow travelled back in time and helped him through the bad years when he was running away from home and refusing to go back.

Chapter 27. **A Memory of my Dad**

LAST NIGHT, I THOUGHT again about my father. He was proud of my Ph.D. He and my sister came to my commencement. I don't know why my mom didn't come. It was a few weeks after my first miscarriage. I hadn't drunk alcohol in a long time throughout my pregnancy. My dad brought me a whopping bottle of Blue Nun wine. I started in immediately, and then we went to the commencement ceremony. Afterwards, we went out to dinner and sat in a lovely corner booth. We all got drunk. As we got up to leave, Jodie and I began laughing about something. My laughter turned to tears as we both slunk down to the floor. I couldn't get up. I just sat there and sobbed. Together we mourned the babies we had lost.

Chapter 28. **A Resolution for my Grandma**

JODIE AND I HAD been shy. This was especially true when we were with my dad's stepmother. After all, we were the bad kids, born of the bad son. So, I was especially surprised when, after her husband died, my grandma gave me her wedding ring. She said it belonged to me, the oldest granddaughter. I never thought I counted as the eldest granddaughter. If I had thought of it, I would have assumed it was going to the good eldest daughter of the good son.

As my grandmother's death approached, my mom and I visited her in her nursing home. As we walked down the halls, my grandmother took me aside. She told me she felt bad about how she treated my father as a child. This totally blew me away, as it was something we had never discussed. I told her what I knew to be true—that my dad wouldn't have wanted her to feel bad about it.

Chapter 29. **Time Spent with my Mother's Sister**

AGAINST UNIMAGINABLE ODDS, MY mom had spent the last several years of her life with her older sister, traipsing around Florida. My favorite auntie and I would go out dancing at a hard rock venue whenever I visited. She would ask me to teach her the lyrics, and we belted them out along with Guns 'n Roses and Metallica. I truly hope that, despite unimaginable odds, my sister and I will someday spend out last years together. We will likely belt out the Beatles!

Dear Paul

Chapter 30. **My OCD**

WE'VE BEEN MARRIED ALMOST fifty years, since 1973. We made it through Nixon (*I'm not a crook!*), Reagan (*welfare cheats!*), and Bush *(the crusade!).* We were together for Cyndi and Sinéad. For Pink Floyd's *The Wall* and Metallica's *Black Album.* We had two children and we lost two baby boys in miscarriages. We completed college and I completed graduate school. You became a musician and I, an economics professor. And I never really told you about myself. You've known something is wrong, but you've never asked me and I've never told you. It is almost too difficult to explain, too hurtful to think about, and just too exhausting. This is why I'm telling you in a letter. It may be a bit disjointed, and it may be piecemeal, but I'll give it a try. I'll try to put it in some chronological order, since my memories are linked to where we lived at the time.

I have obsessive-compulsive disorder. I've had it since I was a young child. People don't talk about their OCD because it's embarrassing. Instead, they try to hide it.

Children don't understand their OCD. They know something is terribly wrong, and they know they are different. Most likely, they think the way I did—that I was stupid. OCD is such a messed-up disorder. I read somewhere it is among the ten most debilitating illnesses in terms of quality of life.

Most people still don't understand it. Of course, my parents noticed something was wrong with me, as did my sister, but they didn't comprehend it any better than I did. We didn't know it was a mental disorder, which would eventually be associated with a diagnosis and treatment. Even if we knew how to talk about it, we certainly didn't talk about things like that in our family. In my family, we pretended everything was fine.

Chapter 31. **The Rules**

THE OCD BEGAN SLOWLY when I was a child. More and more, the rules took over and the darkness surrounded me. These were *my* rules, and I couldn't stop making them. You can't wear your new dress for two full weeks. You have to swim laps instead of swimming for fun. You cannot get out of the pool, even if you're cold or tired, until you've done the required laps. You must play the piano piece over and over, even if you make only one mistake. Same thing with math—do it over and over until there are no mistakes. No pencil. No eraser. You cannot erase—*you have keep doing it over and over.* I remember when the algebra teacher gave an extra-long math assignment, and I put my head down on my school desk and cried. I knew I would never be able to finish it.

There were lots more rules. When you read a book, you must pronounce each word out loud, carefully saying "dot the i" and "cross the t." At the end of the sentence, say either "period" or "question mark." If you turned in one direction while playing tennis, you needed to turn the other way to cancel it out. If you were to swing a tennis racket, it meant you were swearing to yourself, saying "God's name in vain." Swing the racket strong and hard and it meant you were swearing emphatically. It was hard to play well when you had to keep turning and you couldn't swing your racket very hard.

Would you believe that to this day, I still must turn the other way after I've turned in one direction. I need to cancel it out. Everything must be from left to right, and all numerals must end in an even number. Paul, did you ever notice that I always set the television volume to an even number?

The worst part of my OCD was that God was always part of the rules.

Chapter 32. **Hell**

EVERYONE'S OCD IS DIFFERENT, though religious scrupulosity is common. Mine was connected to our Catholicism. I began catechism classes as I entered first grade and I began obsessing shortly after that. I think this is a common age for OCD to kick in for kids. And this was pre-Vatican II, when the rules were strict and the punishment lethal. According to our teachers, hell consisted of burning fire. We were told to think of a burn on our finger, and then imagine our entire body burning forever and ever. Telling this to a child is, of course, a form of child abuse.

And what would send us to hell? Mortal sins, of course. Venial sins were non-lethal but watch out for the mortal sins. You could not receive communion in the state of mortal sin, and if you died in that state, you went straight to hell.

So, what was a mortal sin? Well, there were lots. In my mind, you could commit ten mortal sins before breakfast. Sexual sins were especially mortal. We were told that impure thoughts were mortal sins before we knew what an impure thought was. Better for them to scare us to death before these thoughts even entered the picture. We were told we couldn't touch our private parts. I didn't know what these private parts were. We asked if we could wash these private parts, and we were told we could, but we needed to use a washcloth. We asked if we could scratch these parts and we were told that no, we should not.

To tell a young girl that she must confess all sexual sins to a male priest is also abusive.

And to imagine all those priests who were sexually abusive—well, that just makes me sick.

Chapter 33. **Reassurance**

I NEEDED REASSURANCE. THIS is part of the disorder. So, sometimes I had to ask someone. I would mostly ask my mother. But my questions were so crazy, and she just couldn't cope. *Are you still worried about that? ARE YOU STILL WORRIED ABOUT THAT?!!!* People eventually react to OCD with anger and punishment, which was the case with my family. It is just too hard. It is just too frustrating. It just makes everyone crazy.

Often, my mother expressed utter astonishment that I wasn't "over this" yet. I remember once when Jodie and I took a trip to visit relatives in Canada for two weeks. When we came back, my mom couldn't believe I wasn't better yet. *No mom, this doesn't go away just like that.*

Mostly, my mom just yelled. I yelled back. My dad was normally gentle, but he became furious if I was disrespectful to my mother. He beat me several times. Call it beat or spanked, but whichever it was, it was brutal. It hurt in too many ways. It still hurts.

To other people, OCD is a joke. The hypochondriac. The woman who keeps washing her hands. People who are fearful of dirt, bugs, or diseases. Some people even think it's a good thing. She is such a perfectionist. He gets straight A's. But as everyone with OCD knows, there is nothing good about it. It hurts you. It shatters you. It breaks your mind and it breaks your heart and it breaks the people you confide in. It breaks the very people you need for encouragement and support.

It broke my mom. She screamed a lot. *I hate this. I hate this!*
It broke me. *I Hate It! I Hate It, Hate It, Hate It, Hate It!!*

Chapter 34. **The Professionals**

MY MOM BEGAN TAKING me to see psychologists. One of them must have told her I was doing this for attention and if they would ignore me, it would stop. It didn't stop. We took a family road trip—my family laughing and joking, with me in the back seat all alone and quiet. I was crying softly. No one noticed.

Another psychologist would talk on the phone while I met with him. I would pause, waiting for him to finish. He told me I could just go on talking while he went on talking on the phone . . .

Finally, my mom took me to a psychiatrist, one who could run tests and prescribe meds! He met with me several times, and I thought he was going to help me. But in the end, he told my mom it was just a childhood thing and I would grow out of it. I remember how I cried, as I was counting on him so much to fix me.

There was no diagnosis at the time. There was no treatment. The disease was misunderstood by psychiatrists and therapists alike. They couldn't even see that *no one* has OCD to get attention. We are *embarrassed by our OCD!* My family kept ignoring me and laughing and joking. I was all alone. I cried quietly. No one noticed.

Chapter 35. **The Road Trips**

MY FAMILY TOOK ANNUAL road trips, staying at motels along the way. My favorite things were drive-in restaurants during the day and motels with pools at night. But the rules took over the vacations. Lunch at the drive-in was okay, but I couldn't have the milkshakes I loved. No swimming in the swimming pool. No dessert for dinner.

My parents didn't know how to deal with my OCD. My sister remembers my dad spanking me when I refused to swim in the motel pool. My mom got mad whenever I asked her whether I needed to abide by a rule. Questions like this are common for people with OCD. They seek reassurance. My mom yelled a lot in response. My mom screamed a lot. One time she swore, *god damn it,* then screamed at me and said it was my fault. *Now we have to go to confession and I won't get my house cleaning done!* I guess she had her issues too.

Chapter 36. **Food**

FOOD BECAME A MAJOR issue for me. No eating in-between meals. One spoon of each item for dinner with no seconds. Count the peas. No dessert for dinner. Separate all the food. Don't eat it if it touches. I lost so much weight in those days and I became really skinny.

My Catholic upbringing coincided with the rules. Fast before communion. No eating in-between meals during Lent. No meat on Fridays. How could I brush my teeth on a Friday morning when there might be a morsel of meat on my toothbrush from the night before? How could my Catholic friend splash around doing dishes even though she might get a trace of meat splattered into her mouth? What if the vitamin I took each day was made from meat? What if there was meat on my clarinet mouthpiece when I played it on a Friday? What if I just swallowed some meat by mistake—even though there was no meat and it wasn't even Friday?

Or the Eucharist. What if I sneezed? What if a tiny piece was on my hand, on my papers, on the floor? I would obsessively clean the area, but what about the paper towels I used to clean it? There was really nothing on them, but I put them in a box and saved them. My mom would find them and throw them out. *Such a strange child.*

I will tell you a very sad and embarrassing story, even though it skips around a bit in time, because it is related to this this. The Newman Center church at my graduate school provided the Eucharist in the form of real bread—soft and moist and crumbly bread. Part of what was given to communicants invariably landed on the floor. I took it upon myself to go to church every day before it was vacuumed to pick up the pieces off the floor—the dirty floor from people's dirty shoes. I didn't know what to do with it, so I ate it, crumbs and dirt and all. I did this for what felt like forever. It was a horrible responsibility that was crushing me. It didn't end until we left town.

Chapter 37. **Mortal Sin**

FAILURE TO KEEP ALL the rules meant mortal sin. Mortal sin meant you would burn in hell if you didn't go to confession. And not just the regular church rules, and there were plenty of those. But also, the ones I came up with, the "promises" I made to God as a child. The "vows." Then the "deals." *I'll give up desert if I can eat the popcorn tonight.* But the deals were more like making a new deal to cancel out of a previous deal. Or a previous "vow." *I ate the cookie yesterday so I won't eat one today.* I couldn't stop myself. It was a downward spiral—a spiral down a hole that entangled me and strangled me. Why is it that, up to this very day, I have a reoccurring phrase in my head: *No oaths, no swears, no vows, no deals, no promises, and I'm not under oath.* It had a particular cadence and was ingrained in my brain from all the childhood years when I tried to stop making deals and vows and I just couldn't stop.

I have another built-in phrase that pops out from somewhere deep inside me and into my head every once in a while. *I'm placing you under arrest in the shooting death of your mother.* Yes, that *is* odd. My mom has been dead for a long time now and still this phrase pops into my head.

Chapter 38. **Fixing the Rules**

AS A CHILD, I tried to stop making the promises. I tried to fix them so they didn't count. "I made a deal" with God that any promises I made wouldn't count unless I said them out loud. I had never made a promise out loud, so you would think this would cover it. But what if in my mind I changed the rule? Then there would be a new rule: nothing I promised would count unless I said it out loud on a rug by the door. But what if in my mind I took that back, and then it didn't count unless I said it on a rug by the door with my tennis shoes on. But even then it only counted if I tied my shoes. And, what if I said when I woke up in the morning that "nothing I promise today will count"? I tried that one all the time. But what if I changed it in my mind later on—or at least I thought I did? What about that? And what about all these notes scribbled on my school papers and what if someone sees them? Surely they will know how crazy I am.

I remember the day I heard a scream. I was home alone, lying on the sofa. My head was going through this tangle of OCD and I heard that scream. Then I realized the scream was mine. The shit in my head pushed me over the edge.

Yeah, I knew I was crazy, but like I said, it was more of an opinion that I was stupid, not crazy. I was stupid and different from everyone else. That word I had picked—*stupid*—I use it to this day. It is my "go to." Why can't I fix my bike? *Because I'm stupid.* Why can't I fix my child? *Because I'm stupid.*

Chapter 39. **It Just Got Worse**

MY SYMPTOMS WERE BAD throughout the 1960s, and they only got worse from there. I was in the sixth grade when JFK was killed. My teacher cried when she heard the news, and she sent us home in the middle of the day. Then the Reverend Martin Luther King mesmerized us with his dream. I remember where I was when I heard the news at 6:05 p.m. on April 4, 1968, that he had been shot and killed. Just as I remember the four dead kids at Kent State—immortalized by Neil Young in his song, *Ohio*. I remember Bobby Kennedy and the day he died. I remember when riots tore through Detroit, Harlem, and Watts. Cities were burning down and J. Edgar Hoover ruled the FBI with an iron hand. Mayor Daly did the same in Chicago. People died. In a way they escaped. And by then, my OCD was full-blown.

Dear Paul, Again

Chapter 40. **College**

WE WERE MARRIED IN 1973, two years before we left for graduate school. I know you remember our wedding day. We had the ceremony at the chapel on campus. For the music, a young woman played her guitar and sang for us: *If; Never My Love; In My Life;* and *Here, There, and Everywhere.* We got away with two Beatle songs! Then we drove to my hometown for our reception. Our car broke down on our way to the reception, in the middle of a blizzard. I don't even remember how we got there. No cell phones in those days.

We made it through the next two years. It was easier than before. Living together helped, maybe because no one was watching. No more embarrassment or sobbing in the dark wet grass.

Chapter 41. **Church**

OUR COLLEGE TOWN HAD three Catholic churches. I sought out every priest at every church, over and over, seeking absolution that was never good enough. What did I forget? What did I fail to explain completely? What if I wasn't really sorry? What if I didn't mean it when I promised not to do it again? Every priest in every church—confession, worry, confession, more worry, never enough, never good enough.

The Newman Center priest tried to help me, but he hurt me badly. He gave me a penance. He said to go to Mass and communion two or three times a week for the next four months. It was way too much. I guess he thought if I received communion often enough, I'd get used to it and let go of the associated worries. Sort of cognitive behavioral therapy on steroids. I did the best I could, but we left town for graduate school before the time for the penance was completed. Then life became even harder.

Chapter 42. **Graduate School**

I DECIDED I SHOULD probably continue with all those masses and all that communion, since I hadn't completed the allocated time period. I didn't have time for it, though, and the anxiety about communion only worsened. I would go to church and spend the entire time worrying. Then after communion, I spent all my time thinking I should go to confession. And I didn't have time! Graduate school was intense! The work was harder than anything I had ever done. I didn't have time to waste, but I wasted so much time. So much time in church, worrying, going home and worrying some more.

As you know, Paul, we were living in a large, bustling, and progressive city. Still, it had one extremely conservative Catholic church, another Catholic church in the middle, and a more progressive university Newman Center church. By then life was pretty awful. I was going to church all those times each week, always worrying, always feeling guilty, never doing enough.

I didn't get to communion often enough, so I extended the time of the penance. It went on and on, for years and years. For years and years and years and years . . .

And I kept making rules. I couldn't eat until I decided whether I was in the state of mortal sin. After all, if I had received communion, I had to promise to go to confession. So, I spent all my time thinking about mortal sin before I allowed myself to eat. I went to confession at all the churches. I asked the same questions over and over. I sought the same reassurance. I was never reassured. I sought forgiveness. I never felt forgiven. I sought peace. "Please, God, just give me a little peace." I never received any peace.

Paul, you never went to church with me in those days . . . not until after my first miscarriage. Do you remember? I would come home from church crying because there had been a baptism. That's when you started coming with me. That was nice, Paul.

Chapter 43. **Graduate Work**

WHAT I MOSTLY REMEMBER about school is how hard my studies were. The classes were hard, harder than I'd ever known. I was unprepared. My minor in economics was grossly insufficient, and I hadn't studied math for years. I squeaked. I was lucky. Yet it devastated my self-concept. It wasn't until after I completed my dissertation that I realized mine was so much better than everyone else's. The same was true of my preliminary exams. All those cocky men in the classroom—and they *were* all men—who thought they were so good. They convinced me they were good. And it turns out, I was just as good.

In grad school, no one believed I was really married. They never saw you—not at the parties or other events. Yes, the guys kept hitting on me. My friend Connie was the kind of girl who was always a friend to the boys, but never a girlfriend. All the boys confided in her, and she would tell me whenever some guy was asking about me. And oh, those guys! The French one who offered me wine for lunch. The Italian one who gave up immediately when Connie told him I was married. The Nigerian one who didn't care whether I was married or not.

The first year of graduate school gave me a schedule. Having a schedule helped a little. By the time I was preparing for preliminary exams, and later while working on my dissertation, the work was long and hard, but there no longer was a set schedule. *The lack of a schedule was devastating for me!*

I still had way too much to do, but it didn't require that I be in one place at one point in time. I was going to Mass and communion all the time (and cleaning up everyone's remains). I was seeking out priests on Saturdays. I was taking care of the people I knew who were mentally ill, because, well, I thought that someone had to do it and nobody was. I was thinking and worrying and wasting all my time. My most consuming memory is sitting on the living room floor. All alone or while the babies were sleeping. As I picked at the hair imbedded in the rug, I ruminated endlessly until I could ruminate no more. After hours of thinking and worrying and trying to figure things out, I was no closer to answers than I was before. That's the problem with OCD—it doesn't matter how long and hard you try, how diligently you search, or how many priests or mothers or internet sites you ask, you never really know. In fact, you know less and everything becomes distorted. I later learned that one of the tricks to managing OCD is a willingness to *live with uncertainty*. You are *not* going to figure it out by thinking or asking about it.

And there was the issue of contraception. And parenthood. Artificial contraception was a sin. And postponing childbirth required an important reason. I had an important reason, of course, as I was in graduate school with a plan to save the world from hunger and poverty. But I had to keep rethinking it. Should I stay in school or should I have more babies, day after day, each day for hours, hours that I didn't have? This went on and on and on. Once one issue was finally resolved or forgotten, it was only because a new issue had replaced it.

I tried to take our babies for walks in the stroller, but I always thought I smelled fire or some noxious chemical coming from people's houses. I was sure the residents living there would die unless I checked it out and did something about it. (After all, *someone* had to check on these things. You realize this is OCD talking, yes?) I finally had to stop taking the babies for walks.

You and I fought often. Not physically, thankfully, but we argued and shouted and cried. Everyone knew. It wasn't hard to hear through the walls, the floors and the ceilings, and out into the hallway. Everyone knew.

Our neighbor, Peggy, wrote me a letter many years later. She was angry. She thought I had judged her. She let me know that I was the one who was messed up and not her. Me, Paul, my marriage, my life—that's what was messed up. She said she had always heard us yelling. Always heard me screaming. Always heard me crying. She was right . . . I'll tell you about her.

Chapter 44. **Meeting People**

PEGGY WAS OUR NEIGHBOR across the hall. And she really *was* my friend. She took care of our little boy while I told you about my second miscarriage. At first she was normal. We would drink at night after you went to work, Paul, and she would tell me her stories. I thought she had such an interesting life! Gradually it dawned on me—these stories weren't real. Peggy was bi-polar and would dance outside in the moonlight until I'd say it was time to go to the hospital. She always went willingly. There is nothing stranger than knowing someone, or thinking you know her, and then gradually realizing she isn't real, her stories aren't real, her life as you know it isn't real. It throws you; it causes you to lose your balance.

There were so many others like Peggy.

I met Jane while walking on a bridge. I said hello and she told me her body was broken into many pieces. She meant it literally. It wasn't broken in pieces. I tried to be kind to her, meeting with her often. She had no friends and was schizophrenic. I don't know what eventually happened to her. I visited her in the mental hospital, which was an old and dangerous place. Seriously, *my OCD said I had to.* There were dark stairs and dark halls and minimal supervision and security. But that's what OCD can do to you. It can make you do things that are unsafe, unwise, and certainly not mentally healthy.

I also met Monica. She was bi-polar and schizophrenic, and unlike Peggy, she would never let me take her to the hospital. I first met her at her hotel to interview her as a babysitter for our little boy. She was starving and the hotel was a filthy, unsafe, and horrible place. I knew I needed to take care of her that night. I brought her to our apartment, gave her food and the baby's room, and I took the baby into our room. You were furious. Do you remember? You slept in the car. I didn't sleep. It didn't happen again. But Monica didn't get better. Eventually I set up a police intervention to get her into a hospital, just so she wouldn't starve. She survived and left town, and I didn't know what happened after that until I heard from her sister decades later, telling me that Monica had decided life had become too long.

Paul, I could have used your help with Monica. I could have used your help with the court battle and the police arrangement. With picking up our son up from day care during the episode. And you know those police? They made fun of Monica—pretending they were hitting on her. I asked them not to do that, and they laughed and told me she didn't know what was going on. Of course, she did, and of course it hurt her. Even if she wasn't aware of it, it was still so very wrong.

Except for Simon (who lived down the hall and sold cocaine to a steady stream of unsavory characters), the last person I was faced with was Bonnie. I met her after I completed my doctorate and hadn't made plans for the next phase of our lives. By then we had two children, the littlest just a newborn. I always heard screaming from Bonnie's apartment and I thought she was being abused by her boyfriend. You were working nights and I would let her into our apartment. But then one night, her boyfriend came to our apartment, bloodied and beaten. It turns out *he* was the one being abused. And I had let been letting Bonnie into our apartment with just me and the children all this time!

Sadly, we learned that Bonnie had smothered her baby before we knew her. No one told me until she began hallucinating about my children and I began to inquire. That's when I knew we had to leave.

It was sad and sweet. Bonnie gave me a gift for our baby just before we left. And she advised me to be patient with the baby, and not to give in to anger or impatience when the baby wouldn't stop crying.

Then we left. Life is unkind, and life is unfair. It shouldn't be this hard.

Chapter 45. **The Farmhouse**

THAT WAS WHEN WE moved to the small college town where I taught economics. We first rented a farmhouse and later bought the house in the country where we still live to this day.

I mostly loved the farmhouse, which was large and roomy with seemingly a million bedrooms and unfilled dresser drawers. One could ramble around the house and choose anywhere to land. The only problems were the salamanders and the bathroom. The salamanders lived in the basement and would scramble and run when someone came down and turned on the light. And the bathroom—it was the size of a doghouse and next to the kitchen. It was the only bathroom, and was odd with two doors, one to the kitchen and one to the baby's bedroom. I locked both doors, even though no one else was home. Then I sat on the floor and I cried and cried. I knew my OCD would never get better. If one obsession would go away, it was only because another would replace it. I knew this by now. There was no hope for escape. There was just an overpowering helplessness. Hopelessness. Desperation . . .

This was shortly after we left graduate school, running scared from the crazy woman down the hall. And this was the hardest time of my life, while we lived in the farmhouse.

I wasn't suicidal, since I was a mother. I hated myself though. I hated myself and wanted to hurt myself. I didn't cut, but I scraped my legs with my fingernails until they bled. I hit myself, pounded on myself. I screamed. I cried. I drank.

I didn't get better, not for a long time. At one point I made an important decision though. I knew I would be the only one taking care of myself, so it was up to me to do that. I knew I was harming myself physically and I knew it was related to my drinking. I decided to stop both; stop the drinking and stop the self-harm. *It's remarkable what a decision can do.* I didn't drink anymore and I no longer hurt myself. I've thought about it though—that is, of hurting myself. Whenever I felt a strong loathing for myself, I had visions of stabbing myself. These were automatic images and they occasionally continue to this day. They started with thoughts of stabbing my stomach. Eventually, that changed a bit. After having babies and miscarriages, I switched gears and imagined stabbing myself in the chest. My abdominal area was precious. After all, it was where I had held my babies. This gear switch wasn't intentional, it just was.

I can't talk about my OCD, most of it anyway. I'll give you one of the less embarrassing examples. There was a time when I worried that our marriage wasn't valid. To be as mentally ill as I was when we got married, and to be so emotionally dependent on you, meant that it wasn't really a free choice to marry. I don't know if that automatically invalidated a marriage or if one had to apply for an annulment to make it invalid. I was certain I would receive an annulment if I sought one. Cut and dried. But here's the thing. If our marriage wasn't valid, then I shouldn't have been sleeping with you. Nothing could relieve the horrible anxiety in the pit of my stomach over that worry. What seems so silly now made me feel like the only answer then would be to be dead. Not suicide, just dead. It was that bad.

There was still more to it. The priest who had married us told me earlier that if I was having pre-marital sex, I would have to get married. I was told to choose—marriage or break-up. We know how those "choices" go. I don't think my marriage could have been more forced if there had been a shotgun involved. Just like when the counsellors told me to break-up with you, Paul, I really didn't feel like I had a choice. I got married.

The worry about the validity of my marriage lasted for many years. By that, I mean hours each day, day after day, year after year.

Chapter 46. **The Country House**

EVEN THOUGH MY SENSE of well-being was better after we moved from the farmhouse to the country house, I nevertheless spent a lot of time screaming in this house. It had been a long, long time and I'd just been pushed too far. I hadn't screamed like this since the one time I heard my childself screaming home alone on the sofa, and the other time while lying in the grass in college and the boy came up to see if I was alright. I wasn't alright then and I wasn't alright now.

Our teenage daughter pushed me right up to the edge. So as not to upset the family, I'd get in the car at night and drive and park in the countryside and do that primal scream thing. It didn't help.

Then our son's OCD pushed me over the edge, as it does on-and-off to this day. As you know, I still occasionally scream. Okay, I scream a lot.

I hate it! I hate OCD! *I Hate Everything! It I Hate It I Hate It I Hate It!!!*

Chapter 47. **Those Who Escaped**

JFK, RFK, AND MLK all escaped in the 1960s. It didn't stop there. Jimi and Janis died in 1970. Then Elvis died in 1977 and John Lennon three years later. It just didn't stop. Alternative music arrived and Doug Hopkins of the Gin Blossoms died in 1993. His song title, *Hey Jealousy*, gave us a hint of his alcoholism. Then came grunge, and the death of Kurt Cobain in 1994, which, in my mind, was eerily beckoned in his song titled, *Come as you Are*. In 1995, Blind Melon's Shannon Hoon died. It was, to use his words, "a great escape."

Did you know about John Lennon's round wire-rimmed glasses? Henrick Ibsen was an author I loved as a child. He wrote *Hedda Gabler*, *A Doll's House*, and so much more. I read all his plays. It turns out he loved John Lennon's round wire-rimmed glasses and bought the very same kind. The Ibsen Museum in Oslo tells this story and shows photos of both men wearing their glasses. I had also loved other playwrights, especially George Bernard Shaw. And I read all the Russian authors: Dostoevsky, Tolstoy, Turgenev, Chekhov, and Solzhenitsyn. And as much as I loved to read, it just got so hard when I had to dot the i's and cross the t's. I did eventually see many of their elaborate gravestones in Moscow's Novodevichy Cemetery.

The deaths of the other musicians were sporadic. Layne Staley of Alice in Chains in 2002. Michael Jackson in 2009. Scott Weiland of Stone Temple Pilots in 2015. And what about Prince in 2016, Tom Petty in 2017, and Chris Cornell in 2019? I didn't expect it of Chris Cornell—I thought he was this nice family man who sang about God. Then finally Sinéad. I loved Sinéad. But why did they all escape? Was it all deliberate? Was it careless? I know it wasn't natural.

I don't mean to romanticize these deaths. They are horrible and awful and leave so much suffering in their tracks. I longed for escape, but not this kind. After all, as I say, I'm a mother, and now a grandmother. Besides, this is *not* my plan for escape. My plan is for recovery.

As you know, I've always sung along to hard rock and metal. Well, let's face it—I still do. Of course, Paul, you know this because you always leave the house when I turn on Spotify. But I sang along with musicians and their violent lyrics: Guns n' Roses in their title, *I Used to Love Her*. Jimi in *Hey Joe*. The Talking Heads in *Psycho Killer*. I sang with the haunting lyrics of Queen's *Bohemian Rhapsody*, with Neil Young's title, *I Shot my Baby;* and worst of all, with Pearl Jam's *Jeremy*. That one was too horrible to sing along with, bit I did.

Okay, so I sang along about death and murder. With the exception of *Jeremy*, I didn't give it a second thought. Stone Temple Pilots' *Dead and Bloated*. Megadeath's *Sympathy of Destruction*. It was only music. I think.

Chapter 48. **The Other Deaths**

PAUL, ONLY YOU KNOW how hard I take all the other deaths. Children dying of poverty and hunger. Little kids killed by cluster bombs and assault rifles. Little children lifeless in the Mediterranean. Little kids dead in the Rio Grande . . .

And Black Lives Matter. Remember Michael Brown and Freddie Gray? I sang along with Prince in *Baltimore*: about how "*we're tired of cryin'.*" And Tamir Rice, just a little boy. Unarmed Michael Brown, only eighteen years old. And Elijah, sweet Elijah. Remember how I loved Elijah McClaine? A boy with a sweet disposition who bowed to others so his strangeness wouldn't frighten them. He taught himself to play the guitar and sing to the strays in the animal shelters because he believed it calmed them. And Tyre Nichols. As he cried out for his mother, I cried for her. No mom should see her son's body, beaten and bloodied. And of course, George Floyd. I held a memorial in the city park for him. Paul, you helped me put up the poster and arrange the flowers. We did the same for Mahsa Amini, for Shireen Abu Akleh, for the victims of Uvalde, El Paso, Tree of Life, and Mother Emanuel AME . . .[1]

---

1. Iranian Mahsa Amini was killed for wearing her hijab improperly and Shireen Abu Akley was a Palestinian-American journalist killed by an Israeli sniper. Uvalde refers to the school shooting at Robb Elementary School, El Paso was the location of the mass killing of Hispanics, the Tree of Life Synagogue known for the mass killing of Jewish worshippers, and Mother Emanuel AME Church remembered for the mass killing of Black parishioners.

Why don't people die like they're supposed to? Why don't they die of old age, or cancer, or a heart attack? Why is it with a gun, a chokehold, a drug, an addiction, or a cold unwillingness of anyone to give a damn?

And then came 2003 . . .

Chapter 49. **The Invasion of Iraq**

IT WAS THE BUILD-UP to the war in Iraq. I worked with people from the Middle East, and they explained how deadly and ineffective a war would be. There would be so much suffering, suffering that we would cause and wouldn't end soon.

I didn't trust our government. Not when the vice president was closely linked to Halliburton, the company that would benefit financially from the war. Not when the president was a cowboy who talked with the gusto of the crusaders. Not when anyone who paid close attention knew there were no weapons of mass destruction, or WMD as we called them.

I mobilized the campus together with the local community, something no one had done in a long, long time. (I had done it once before, in 1991, just before Operation Desert Storm.) I developed a list-serve with hundreds of names and email addresses. We marched every Monday afternoon, and regularly nourished our souls with potlucks at the campus ministry building. We were dedicated and determined.

Against all advice, I went on the radio talk show of a rightwing host who manipulated his show and everyone on it. I defeated him soundly. I organized teach-ins for the entire campus. I invited speakers to classrooms. I wrote letters and editorials. I became a "celebrity" on campus and in the community.

I also became a target. I was harassed by the Young Republican student organization. They stalked me. They came upon me alone in the dark. They assaulted me verbally as I walked past them at night. They wrote lies about me in the student newspaper and drew ridiculous political cartoons to denigrate me. That part was hard, but I wasn't a victim. I just kept going.

My side lost, and the U.S. invaded Iraq in 2003. But I had kept myself busy. All that is what helped save me from my OCD.[1]

1. I apologize if my politics offend you. I've written from my heart, and unfortunately, my heart includes a great deal of skepticism about war and other social issues. I do not mean to cause offense to you if you disagree with me, I especially ask your forgiveness if I've hurt you in any way about your service in these wars or the service of your friends or family. You and others were certainly engaged in a good faith effort and I hope you can find it in you to bear with me.

Chapter 50. **My Dad Died**

I WAS AT A conference when my mom phoned me. *Can you get on the next flight? You dad is dying.*

We were expecting this, we just didn't know when.

My dad died in November 1994, exactly nine months after the doctor accurately predicted his death. My mother's fantasies about the long and happy life were just that—fantasies to avoid the pain.

It was an extraordinarily peaceful death. My sister and I moved in with my mom and dad that final week, and we all took turns being with him. I often took the night shift and ended up in bed with him. I would hold his legs so they wouldn't be "restless." As the end approached, the three of us sat around him on the bed. He was unconscious. Even though my dad wasn't Catholic and my sister hadn't practiced in years, my mom asked if we could hold hands and say the "Hail Mary." Of course, we obliged. I said the words thoughtfully, and realized we'd been saying these words all our lives. *Holy Mary, mother of God, pray for us now and at the hour of our death.* Somehow, I found that enormously comforting.

After his death, I went to sit in the living room. My dad's body no longer meant anything to me, as he was no longer there. My mom phoned the funeral home to pick up his body. She also phoned the hospice people. But first, she took a bowl of water and soap and carefully washed his entire body, the body she had always loved. The body that would be cremated in just a few hours. In so many ways, my mom showed me what love is.

Chapter 51. **I Nearly Died**

IN 2005, I HAD surgery. Unbeknownst to anyone, it left me with a fistula. I've never been able to visualize a fistula, so I can't explain exactly what it is. I do know what it means, though. It means bodily fluids can be exchanged from one body part to another. Medical professionals refer to this fluid exchange rather oddly as "communication." I went home after the surgery and had sporadic mild fevers. The third time it went over 102 degrees, I called the doctor and he said I'd better come in. The CT scan showed my abdominal cavity was entirely filled with strep infection. Somehow, I had minimal symptoms. They quickly placed me on powerful IV antibiotics and sent me by ambulance to a major hospital that was far more capable of treating me and my outsized infection than my small-sized local hospital.

I survived.

They fixed me.

Except they didn't.

The next time, my abdominal cavity filled with a staph infection. Same emergency procedures as the last time.

And then, a third time—this time, the worst. My abdominal cavity was filled with a fungal infection. I say the worst because the anti-fungal treatment made me sick. They sent me home, but I couldn't keep the medication down. They had to put me on IV-treatment at home. I just kept vomiting. I couldn't keep down food or water. I grew weaker and weaker. My skin turned to scales and my hair fell out. I was too weak to walk and would pass out when I stood.

My husband took me back to the doctor and he ran some blood tests and sent me home. The blood draw took a long, long time because by then, my body was jerking sharply and spastically and my veins were shot. When I finally got home, my doctor phoned. *Come right back to the hospital. Your kidneys are failing.*

All in all, I had eight abdominal surgeries. I had multiple infections, including antibiotic-resistant infections like MRSA and VRE. I had exactly one million intestinal obstructions and if you know what childbirth is like, then you get the picture. It involves a lot of writhing and screaming. I was lucky to survive it all.

Chapter 52. **My Mom**

THERE IS MORE TO this story. It involves my mom. My mom came to take care of me whenever I was sickest. She told me that men can help, but they don't know how to fluff pillows. She made me homemade vegetable broth when that was all I could eat. She made me homemade oatmeal when I was in the hospital eating "hospital oatmeal." She grieved for me when we thought I was dying. She was just so good to me. I will never forget this. To this day, I cannot say bad things about my mom (this true confession excepted), as all the other things just seem so unimportant now. This one more time, she taught me what love is.

My mom died when I was fifty-eight years old. I was cheated out of being with her, the way I was when my dad died. She had a heart attack and died instantly. There were five states between us. My sister and I mourned together. We had become orphans.

When we held the funeral service, so many people told us how much they loved our mom. Of course, we had expected that. But people also told us there was an error in the obituary. Her age was correctly listed as eighty-three, but no one believed she was over sixty-five. She was beautiful at the time she died, as she had been all her life. And by the last years of her life, she was warm and soft.

Chapter 53. **The Depth of my Pain**

PAUL, YOU KNOW THAT underlying all the sadness and death and wars that I wrote about is about the depth of my own pain. My pain over my life, the lives of our children, and all the lost time. The desperation. The hopelessness. The helplessness. But I want you to know I am recovering. You will soon see how I got here. And that is the best part of this story!

Recovery

Chapter 54. **The Need for Certainty**

I AM NOT AN authority on OCD. I'm not an expert on therapy or medication. I don't know what it's like for other people with OCD and I don't know how they get past it, if they get past it. If not, I don't know how they survive it, if they survive it. I do know they have different kinds of issues. They worry about harm they may have caused, or sexual sins they may have committed, or diseases they may acquire. I think their issues are ridiculous and they think that mine are. Whose issues are the most ridiculous?[1] I imagine this is a common topic amidst many OCD support group sessions. We always think our issues are the worst. On some level, *we know they aren't real.* And the ones that are real are *vastly* exaggerated in significance by our OCD. And then the next one comes along. This one seems worse than all the others. We think that maybe this one *is* real. *The last one always tells us it is real.* This goes on until the next one comes along. I totally get all that.

We can't always control the terrible feelings associated with our issues—for me, the horrible anxiety and guilt associated with my OCD. The self-doubt and self-loathing. And the helplessness and hopelessness—the belief that I would aways have this horrible feeling

---

1. I don't mean to make fun of anyone and their OCD. I am just using this idea to point out that what may seem very real to us doesn't make sense to others.

in the pit of my stomach. This horrific feeling about an issue that would never go away until a different one arrived to replace it.

It is so hard to live with these feelings. It is so hard to live with uncertainty. There are all the "what ifs." *What if it is real? What if it's a mortal sin? What if it will send me to hell?* I don't think I worried as much about hell as I worried about confession. *What if it's a mortal sin and I have to go to confession?* The "what ifs." And the "yeah buts." *Yeah, but, this one might be real. Yeah, but, I should probably go to confession.*

We need to know that all the confession and all the reassurance does not help. We need to know that all the thinking and all the googling does not help. They feed our OCD, giving it oxygen, enabling it to thrive. That is why we have to decide to live with uncertainty. That is why we have to decide to live with self-doubt. Eventually, without oxygen, the OCD will die, and eventually, along with it, the doubt and anxiety.

Note that I said, *we have to decide*. Decisions are separate from feelings. We can be filled with anxiety and uncertainty, yet we can still make decisions. Let me tell you about my decision.

Chapter 55. **The Need for Decisions**

THE GOOD NEWS IS *that even if we can't control our feelings, we can at least make decisions and stick with them.* This was my wisest discovery, and perhaps the best advice I can offer you.

At first, I decided to only go to confession one or two times per year, at least six months apart. I told this to my priest and he said he thought this was fine and I should feel free to continue to receive communion. He approved, and therefore confirmed my decision. It was a good one. After all, it accomplished a major goal. There was no more need to spend endless hours fixated on whether or not I committed a mortal sin, since it would have no bearing on my decision about confession and communion. It was hard, but doable.

But it didn't entirely work. There were setbacks, and then more and more until it was becoming just like the old days.

When I was seventy years old, a wise old lady indeed, I decided it was time for my freedom. I wanted to live, and I wanted to enjoy the rest of my life. I may have only ten, twenty, or thirty years left, and I want to make the best of them. I decided to go all the way.

I made a choice, driven by necessity, something I should have done long ago. I didn't assess and analyze this choice, and I tried not to ever look back. I didn't know whether it was right or good. I don't know if it was morally acceptable, or permissible within the confines of Catholicism. I truly believe we have to stop caring about all that.

Do something even if it's wrong. Trust it to your instincts, or to the universe, or to God—to anything! Just trust it.

I went to the same priest, someone who understood mental illness, unhappiness, and the need for freedom. Over all these years, he had known how I suffered. *So, I didn't ask him—I told him.* I said I couldn't live this way any longer. I couldn't live with the rules. Confession, penance, Mass, sorry for this and sorry for that, promises to do better, should I go or should I not, should I confess or should I not?

I told him I was finished with the church's rules. Church rules meant I couldn't breathe. They meant a constant dread in the pit of my stomach. They meant I might be horribly bad.

My OCD had kept me from being the mother I wanted to be, the wife I wished I could be. It kept me from being happy. I was busy, but not very happy.

I think it is the uncertainty that makes us crazy. Did I sin? Should I go to confession? Can I receive communion? Should I think about this and figure it out? Should I literally spend hours thinking, sometimes reading about it, often searching the internet? All that time and all that angst, and I was always left with that horrible feeling in the pit of my stomach. I was uncertain. And because I was uncertain, I was "bad." Because I never resolved it. Because I couldn't. All those hours and I never resolved anything.

Along with the rules, I threw out confession. *This was the most important decision I ever made.* Again, I don't know if this was moral or good, but it was the only thing I could do. After all, the reassurance that should come from confession never arrived (amidst all those "what ifs" and "yeah buts"). More importantly, confession is a form of "checking," the seeking of reassurance that is the heart of OCD. In many ways, reassurance isn't the answer; and with OCD, it can make things worse. In the same way, we will never find that certainty we search for. We just have to accept that we will live with the uncertainty of the unknown and uncontrolled. *It does get easier.*

The priest knew all that about me. He encouraged me. He agreed—no more rules. No more confession. He sent me off to a brand-new life, a life that now includes my joyful presence at church, me and the other "misfits" way in the back who mutter when the priest calls us brothers, who play with the entirely bored children, who share in the Eucharist, and who love each other like family.

Chapter 56. **The First Day of the Rest of my Life**

THAT WAS THE FIRST day of the rest of my life. I'm not sure why this time was different. I had "first days of the rest of my life" for decades, written about them in my journals that were intended to encourage me and keep me going, but they never did. *Nothing* had ever helped me before. This time turned out to be different, not perfect, but so very different. The difference was that I made a decision and I stuck with it. I made a decision and I didn't look back.

I beg you to do the same. Despite all your doubts and uncertainties, and despite the anxiety it may cause, *make a decision to choose mental health.* If your worrying, checking, seeking reassurance, googling, or anything else you are doing is bad for your mental health, decide not to do it! Don't regret the past and don't worry about the future. Once your mental health is restored, the future will fall in place and erase or heal the regrets of the past. In time, you will also find that your doubts, uncertainties, and anxiety will dissipate. This is how it worked for me.

Chapter 57. A Vicious Malevolent Thing

AN OCD BRAIN IS a terrible thing. It is spiteful, malicious, venomous, and cruel. It is sadistic, vindictive, inhuman, and inhumane. It is so damn smart. It knows where to find the triggers and how to arrange the links. It knows how to take its tentacles and wrap them just right to make you crazy and crazier. It digs deeper and deeper, in circles and in twists, and more and more until it breaks your brain. And then it comes back, and it starts again, and again, and again. It is smart because it knows you, and it knows you because it *is* you. It is *your* brain.

We have to kill it.

Just like I had two dads: a real dad and a drunk one, we have two brains: a real brain and a sick and distorted one. We have to take our real brain, the good brain, and use it to gather up all the OCD—all its tentacles and its slime, all its viciousness and venom, and put it all in a great big sack and just throw it all over the damn cliff. Don't worry whether everything belongs in the sack . . . just throw it all over. No "what ifs . . ." No "yeah buts . . ." Just throw it all over. Let it go. Feel the freedom. Feel the breeze. Flap your wings and fly away. Never go back. Never look back.

Chapter 58. My Work Helped Me

EVEN BEFORE MY RECOVERY, it was my work that helped me. It provided a schedule I had to keep. It meant interaction with people that kept me from thinking about other things. It meant teaching classes, attending meetings, and preparing lectures. I later started writing grant proposals, almost maniacally. I was successful in all of them—well, all of them but one. It seems no one wanted to pay my expenses to travel to Paris to brush up on my French before traveling to West Africa, where the common language is French. But all my other grant proposals were funded. One year I wrote fourteen successful grants. How would I do all the work I just got funded?

I just kept going. The grants paid for research and projects abroad, and I traveled across Africa, Asia, Latin America, and Europe for research and consulting. The knowledge I gained and shared was well worth the grant money. The grants also paid for campus projects that benefited students of minority race and ethnicity. I wrote a grant proposal to establish a Center for International Development, bringing together faculty from different disciplines to put our heads together for the world's poor. The grants paid for videos and discussion groups that I offered across campus—videos about exploitation, fair trade, world poverty, and so much more. And every year I sponsored a World Food Day Program and a Center for International Development Conference.

Once I volunteered to organize "International Education Week." I put together a schedule of local and outside speakers, authors, researchers, activists, and so on, and I filled every minute of every day. In the evenings, I provided videos and films. It was my craziest week ever. I didn't leave a minute here or a minute there for me (or anyone else) to rest.

I was advisor to the Student Economic Society, the Socialist Student Organization, and Amnesty International. I directed the International Development Center and I had a second office in International Affairs. If a nice big corner office with large outside windows on two walls and a three-screen computer on a lovely desk are signs of success, then I was successful indeed.

My social justice activity also helped me. It gave me comradery, it gave me confidence, and it helped fill my time and my mind. That is why I've written so much about it. All of this helped me.

Chapter 59. **If You Have OCD**

I DON'T KNOW YOU, and I don't know your OCD. Still, I want you to know I care about you. I care about you *so* much. I hope I've helped you, at least a little, hopefully a lot. You know that you are not in this alone, and I want you to get well. I can tell you a few more things I've learned over my lifetime.

Maybe most importantly, everyone is hurting in some way. My adult child looks through the lighted windows along the dark streets and imagines everyone inside is happy. I remember how I used to do that too. I explain that things are not as they appear. Everyone is at least partially broken. Each of us struggles. And, contrary to what we all might have been led to believe, life is never easy.

Secondly, as I indicated, it is important it is to stay busy, to have some sort of schedule, and to interact with people. These are so important for keeping your mind off your OCD. Staying home in bed will not help you feel better. There is no magic in the world that will create recovery while you're lying in bed. It really does take our own hard work.

As I've described myself, it is probably pretty clear that I've been overly active. *No one* writes fourteen grants in one year, fills in every minute of International Education Week, or takes their computer to bed with them. But I do and it helps me. I also learned that if I enjoy the things I do to keep busy, then I have things to look forward to as well. This helps reduce the power of hopelessness.

You don't have to do all that. But you have to do something. Take a walk. Interact with someone. Go to the store. Or just do whatever you can do. It doesn't need to be something monumental. Just something little . . .

Third, we really don't have to be perfect. We don't even have to come close. I remember something a wise old woman once said. I had told her I planned on walking for thirty minutes every day. Later she asked if I'd been walking, and I said no—I just couldn't do thirty minutes every day. She said that sounds like someone with OCD, someone who thinks they must do it all, and do it perfectly, and do it all the time, or just not bother. Somehow I remembered that. If I don't get to walk as much or as often as I think I should, I just do what I can, when I can, and it's okay.

Fourth, it's important to get the help you need from a good psychiatrist, perhaps medication, and a good therapist. I was lucky to find a therapist who understands OCD. That said, even a mediocre therapist just might ask the right questions and you will find you already know the answers. We often know the answers, but it helps to say them out loud to someone. And, sometimes just talking can help. But if your psychiatrist or therapist says the *wrong* things, the things that make everything worse, be sure to tell them that. I say this from knowing someone with that experience. Let me explain.

One common concern of people with OCD is their fear that they don't really have OCD. What if a psychiatrist, or therapist, or friend, or anyone . . . suggests to them that maybe they have some other illness, maybe ADHD or generalized anxiety, but not OCD? This can be traumatizing, because if they don't have OCD, it must mean that all their worries are real. And that would be horrible. It would confirm all their worst fears. *Please don't go there. You have OCD. You know you do. You know all your worries are OCD.* Don't question yourself. And while it's certainly possible to have more than one mental disorder, you still have OCD and all your worries are still OCD.

Fifth, it may be helpful to explain your disorder to close friends. You always run the risk of being stereotyped and therefore not taken seriously (or worse yet, blamed for things like a failed relationship). But good friends will likely be supportive and helpful. My dear friend knows how I've struggled with OCD. Whenever a new random priest talks about sin or confession in his sermon, my friend traipses across the church, finds me, hugs me, and tells me it is okay. *Always remember the wisdom of wise old ladies!*

It also may be helpful to explain your disorder to the professionals you deal with, such as your doctor or employer. They can be helpful and perhaps avoid saying the wrong things. (You may have to tell them what these things are.) Again, there is a risk of being stereotyped and therefore not taken seriously or blamed for things. There is also the risk of losing your job.

Sixth, maybe a mediated OCD support group can help. I've never tried this, but I can see how it could be good—all those people with OCD telling you your issues are not real. You might check out the International OCD Foundation (www.iocdf.org) for their resources and information on therapists and support groups.

And finally, please don't give up. Look—it took me until I was seventy years old and fighting against the Catholic Church no less. But if I can do it, you can do it. (And you really don't have to wait until you're seventy years old.) Do it now. And most importantly, don't take those awful escapes—don't romanticize them and don't consider them. Your life is far too precious for that. And I care about you. I care very much. We are in this together, and we *stay* in this together.

Chapter 60. **A Few More Thoughts**

I HAVE A FEW more thoughts for those of you with OCD. First, recovery from OCD doesn't make life easy or solve all your problems. Unfortunately, life can be hard and some of the problems may still exist. This is especially true for those with a child with OCD, which I'll return to momentarily. But, your own recovery will help you get through the hard times.

Also, I know you may be struggling with additional issues that make your recovery more difficult than mine. I apologize if I've seemed callous or oblivious to this. Along with OCD, you may have debilitating depression that keeps you bed, incapacitating anxiety that keeps you from leaving home, or medical constraints that make life even so much harder. Your life may be complicated by abuse, addictions, homelessness, PTSD, or so much else. You may lack of effective treatment (due to financial or insurance restrictions, remote location, unavailable professionals, or just the inability to find "the right" psychiatrist, therapist, treatment program, and/or medication). If so, I'm so sorry.

The last two are difficult and I'll admit that I've been there. It may be hard enough to find a qualified professional, and so much harder to find one with whom you have some rapport. Some psychiatrists and therapists can be a poor fit for you, lack the "proper" temperament for you, and in some cases, even say to you the "wrong" things I referred to earlier.

And finding the right medication can be particularly tough. Building the full effectiveness of a medication can take time.

There can be debilitating side effects that may or may not go away over time. And you may require a combination of medications and struggle with the proper dosing. Needless to say, you really need an excellent psychiatrist and a lot of support. Keep talking with your doctor or find a new one if necessary. Even your primary care physician can be a great secondary support.

On the positive side, I've been told that cognitive behavioral therapy (CBT) has been shown to be as effective as medication, if not more so. The combination of meds and CBT may be especially helpful for you.

All of these complications may make you feel hopeless about your recovery. I really do understand that. But you have to try. You have to want it and want it badly. It isn't going to be easy. But I believe it is doable. Please know that you are in my heart as you struggle to get there.

Chapter 61. **One More Thing**

I WANT YOU TO know that I've accomplished considerable success in life, despite my OCD. I don't say this to brag, but to let you know it is possible. And success comes in lots of different ways. Remember all those folks in the living room windows that we all assume are perfectly happy? It's just not true. *Everybody Hurts.* Even if all we do is smile or be kind in some small way, it can be hugely important to someone else.

I want you to smile and be kind because the OCD feelings of helplessness are what makes this disorder so disabling, leaving us bereft of any hope for the future. It doesn't have to be that way, and you *can* get better—but in the meanwhile, I want you to know you can achieve huge success with simple acts of kindness. Keep track of *all* your accomplishments, even if it is "just" getting up and out of bed. Even if you don't stay up for all that long. Maybe you will find you can stay up for just a little longer each day. And if you slide, you can always get up again. You are not alone in this.

And please remember—I spent my life making and keeping rules. *But there are no rules.* There! How does that feel? You are free to be the person you want to be. If it's OCD that held you back, then toss your OCD. You have my permission and my blessing. And by the way, the awful feeling of dread does eventually go away. After a while, your decision becomes a lifestyle, and with it, a much better sense of the person you really are. There is joy and hope and satisfaction.

Chapter 62. **If Your Child has OCD**

THE WORST THING ABOUT OCD is that it can be genetic. In my opinion, this is life's greatest unfairness. I mentioned that I have a child with OCD. It was evident in the farmhouse, when my child went from happy and energetic, to quiet, thoughtful, distracted, and eventually near catatonic. My little one began to say only a few words: *mom, I'm so worried*. My child slept on the sofa. I brought him food. I held him. It didn't get better. We took him to a psychiatrist, who gave him a diagnosis, and prescribed a medication. It helped for many years. There were no psychiatrists for me, not yet anyway, and no medications. I cannot talk much about my child's OCD, as that is not my story to tell. There are better times, and there are worse times.

I thought I could help my child because I had gone through it. I wasn't going to yell in the ways of my mom or be violent in the ways of my dad. And at first I could do that, stay calm and helpful and get my child the needed professional assistance. That's important for a parent with a child with OCD.

But my child with OCD is now an adult with OCD, and for me, it's been far too much for far too long and I can no longer cope that well with it. Sometimes I scream when the phone rings. Sometimes I rant when I get off the phone. Frankly, I wonder why I haven't yet killed the phone.

Sometimes, the harder I try, the more I end up screaming. And ranting. And crying. And screaming some more.

I understand about enabling, about being there at the beck and call for reassurance about OCD. I understand about how we cannot fix our adult children; they have to do it for themselves. I understand these things intellectually. Living them is a bit different.

One time, I just gave up on worrying about enabling. I phoned my child and said I was coming over. I was bringing food. I had all the phone numbers and would make all the calls—the hospitals, the doctors, the therapists, the programs, the insurance, the county offices . . . I would talk to everyone, yell at them if I had to, and demand that they fix my child!!! Then I would hand the phone to my child, and voila!

I was ready to do that. I cooked the food, had my phone list, and was ready to go. And then my child phoned me and told me not to come. He was feeling very bad and going back to bed. I hung up. And I started screaming. I'm still surprised I didn't kill the phone.

If your child has this disorder, I am so very sorry. I encourage you to get help for yourself and the rest of your family (it *does* affect the other kids and your marriage). I just can't tell you how to fix your child. I wish that I could, but I don't know how. One thing I know is it that it helps if you ask your child to promise that no matter how bad it gets, he or she *will not commit suicide*. His promise has helped me get through all the times that he admitted to me that his greatest wish was for death.

Maybe it isn't for us to figure out how to fix our adult children. Maybe they have to fix themselves, but what if they can't or won't? I know we can't let ourselves go crazy over it, but I find myself doing that anyway. Maybe all we can do is be there when they need our support and offer them our love and advice.

My child did eventually write a phone list, contact a psychiatrist and therapist, and is now trying an adjunct to current medication. Things are moving slower than we would like, but we are moving forward. I know it sounds like I've failed at my own recovery, with all the screaming and ranting and urges to kill the phone. But that isn't the case at all and I'm in such a better place for myself. I do have times of joy, peace, celebration, and wonder. And despite my struggles with my child, I no longer live with helplessness, but I thrive on hope.

Chapter 63. **If You're in an Unhealthy Romantic Relationship**

MY RELATIONSHIP WITH PAUL was unhealthy. The dependency, the fighting, the emotional abuse . . . If these are your experiences, they are signs you need to leave. Get the help you need to do it, but just make sure that you leave. I know it isn't just that easy, especially with kids and not much money. But look for friends, family, or a shelter that can help you with both.

I didn't take that advice. My marriage and life with my husband are good right now, but if I could change things, I would have done it differently. There has just been too much hurt—for me, for him, and for our kids—and for far, far too many years. I was lucky in the end. Most people are not.

Chapter 64. **An Optimistic Note**

AFTER I CUT BACK on trying to fix things for my child, one amazing thing did happen. My husband stepped in. Not to yell at or criticize our child, but to calmly advise and encourage and appreciate him. I never expected this from the man I always fought with over how to treat our child. Maybe it will help.

There is one other thing—I described how my mother cared for me while I was sick. Actually, so did Paul. He drove hours every day to visit me in the hospital. He brought me the *New York Times* each day, even when I was near-comatose. He picked me up when I fell down. He walked me, practically carried me, when I had to move around in the house. He grew vegetables that he made into a juice blend because I could drink but couldn't eat vegetables. He helped me with the medical technology that involved far more amateur home nursing than I ever imagined they would let us undertake. And when I wanted to give up, he took over the medical technology and everything else and just did it all for me. He tried to cheer me, he got me through it, and like my mother, he taught me what love is.

Now, I'm not going to take back what I said in Chapter 64. I still want you out of a bad relationship. But somehow I was lucky, and against what I assume were all the odds, my marriage eventually worked out. My husband is truly a good man.

Chapter 65. **Notes on my Writing**

I'VE PLACED A LOT of my own personal circumstances in this book, including for context the music I sing, the books I read, and the people and politics that affect me. These include a lot of people who have died for unnatural reasons. The music lyrics are random—I've always sung along to lyrics and had an affinity for hard rock and metal. I think the music calms me, something like all that noise was calming to my mom. But the deaths of musicians upset me. I want to emphasize that I *do not* romanticize death by suicide or drug overdose. I don't *ever* want anyone to make that choice.

Lastly, I already mentioned the *International OCD Foundation* at www.iocdf.org. I strongly encourage you to visit their site, whether you have OCD or you are just wondering, or whether you have an affected family member or friend. This organization has tons of informative resources and can help you connect with the help you need, including moderated OCD support groups.

Chapter 66. **My Theology**

THE PRIEST WHO HELPED me told me he envisions the Holy Spirit as female. I picture her as a wise old lady. I picture myself as a wise old lady as well. Surely, I have lived long enough to experience life. And surely I've been paying attention. My seventy-two years of experience with life, with children and grandchildren, with love and hate, with my own mental torment and that of my child . . . it has to count for something.

I don't have a sophisticated theology. The rules might be good, or they might be bad. I'm sure they're good for some people. They are bad for me. They're bad for my mental health, and it's just that simple. And I'm not going back to them. Sometimes, I start to slip and I think, well maybe just this time. What if this thing I did actually was the *really bad thing,* the one thing for which I should go to confession. What if . . . ?

No, I'm not going back.

I do believe in God. Amidst all that screaming—I hate OCD, I hate myself, I hate everything, I hate everything! *I Hate It Hate It Hate It Hate It . . .* I think there must have been anger at God, maybe even hate. Why is life so unfair? Why is it so hard? Why is there OCD? Why does my child suffer so much? Or for that matter, why do other people suffer? Despite my best efforts, why is there *still* global hunger and poverty?

I know. *Free will.* I get it. We have free will, so someone might choose to hurt someone else, let's say to be cruel to a poor person. But that's not fair. Why should a mother and child suffer from poverty because someone has the free will to harbor their contempt for the poor? If I was God, it wouldn't be that way. There'd be no suffering, regardless of free will.

And I also know—*we* are the hands of God. Where there is suffering, *we* are the ones to fix it. That is what Jesus desperately tried to tell Peter, three times before he died: *Peter, do you love me? Then feed my sheep.* [Paraphrased, from John 21:15-17.] But again, this isn't fair. Why should the poor mother and child suffer because I've decided not to do what Jesus asks, what He begs us to do?

And lastly, what about the pain caused by natural disasters and accidents? What about the pain caused by disorders like OCD?

I believe in molecules. I believe we were created by science, and at some point a God of love slipped in and gifted us with a soul, a spirit—a soul and spirit of love, given and received and lived in completely and fitting like a glove. And I believe in Jesus, because I believe in the words He said and the things He did. The person He was while on earth, and the God He was when He promised to be with us always. He sees all our pain and shares our tears. He agrees with me on all the important things. We both care about the poor and suffering. And, I believe in the Holy Spirit, who as I said, is a wise old lady like me. Together, we rock.[1]

I just don't understand the world. I don't understand the pain and the power, but it isn't for me to understand. My bare bones theology has to be enough. If I were pushed, I guess I would agree with the great rabbi Harold Kushner, author of *When Bad Things Happen to Good People.*[2] He wrote that it is inconsistent that God is both all loving and all powerful, or the holocaust would not have occurred. I choose to believe that God is all loving.

Now I live. I like to write. I can do it in bed with my computer on my lap. I'm writing in bed right now. And licking my lips. And wearing my Guns 'n Roses T-shirt. You should see me!

---

1. I apologize to those who are not Christian and I hope I am not offending you. I am merely writing from my own deep faith and I deeply respect yours.

2. Kushner, *When Bad Things Happen to Good People.*

I also like to paint, and I keep my paint supplies at the ready. I turn on Spotify and along with Sinéad, I belt out her title, *Nothing Compares 2 U!*

Chapter 67. **Musicians and Music Titles**

John Lennon and Plastic Ono Band, *Give Peace a Chance.* Bread, *If.* Cat Stevens (Yusuf), *It's a Wild World.* Led Zeppelin, *Stairway to Heaven.* Neil Young, *Don't Let it Bring you Down.* Laura Nyro, *"Gonna kill . . . my Lover-Man"* in *Tom Cat Goodbye.* Songs sung by Jodie and me: The Beatles: *Let it Be, All My Loving,* and *She Loves You;* The Mama's and the Papa's, *California Dreamin';* Petula Clark, *Downtown;* Sonny and Cher, *I've Got You Babe;* and Herman's Hermits, *Mrs. Brown You've Got a Lovely Daughter* and *I'm Henry the Eighth I Am.* Neil Young *(Ohio).* Cyndi is Cyndi Lauper and Sinéad is Sinéad O'Connor. Wedding songs: Bread, *If;* The Association, *Never My Love;* The Beatles, *In My Life* and *Here, There, and Everywhere.* Jimi is Jimi Hendrix, Janis is Janis Joplin, and of course, Elvis is Elvis Presley. Nirvana (Kurt Cobain), *Come As You Are.* Blind Belon (Shannon Hoon), *"It's a great escape"* in *No Rain.* Guns n' Roses (Axl Rose), *I Used to Love Her.* Jimi Hendrix, *Hey Joe.* The Talking Heads, *Psycho Killer.* Queen (Freddie Mercury), *Bohemian Rhapsody.* Neil Young, *Down by the River.* Pearl Jam, *Jeremy.* Prince, *"we're tired of cryin'"* in *Baltimore.* Guns 'n Roses (Axl Rose), *Sweet Child O' Mine.* R.E.M.: *Everybody Hurts.* Sinéad O'Connor, *Nothing Compares 2 U, Mandinka, Famine, Black Boys on Mopeds.*

Bibliography

Bread for the World, www.bread.org.

International OCD Foundation, www.iocdf.org.

Kushner, Rabbi Harold, *When Bad Things Happen to Good People,* NY: Anchor, 1981.

Sheehan, Neil, et al. *The Pentagon Papers: The Secret History of the Vietnam War,* NY: Skyhorse, 2018. © New York Times.